What Readers Are Saying About
Every Young Woman's Battle
by Shannon Ethridge

"*Every Young Woman's Battle* is shockingly h[...] which is exactly what this generation needs. I thi[...] the perfect approach in dealing with some sensitive topics. The result is a very true, honest, and effective look at issues facing young women today."

— SARAH KELLY, recording artist for Gotee Records

"Like a steady IV drip, today's teenage girls get a message of confused and cheapened sexuality. They are desperate for reasons to guard and preserve themselves. Shannon Ethridge gives girls reasons in this relevant and readable book. Every young woman and every young woman's mother need to read this book!"

— SHARON HERSH, author of *"Mom, I Feel Fat!"* and *"Mom, I Hate My Life!"*

"I'm so grateful that Shannon decided to be as honest and real as she is— that's the only way this book could be as powerful as it is.… God is going to heal in unbelievable ways through this potent work of art and heart!… I can honestly say that this book has changed me—because it gives a clear picture of who Jesus is, who we are as His bride, and why we can't seem to be satisfied with anything or anyone else."

— BETHANY DILLON, songwriter and recording artist

"A must-read for every teenage girl! Honest and informative, this book is not only highly readable with its true-to-life illustrations, but it's packed with answers for every sexual situation today's teens encounter. What a great antidote for the twisted sexual messages our pop culture continues to dish out. Way to go, Shannon!"

—MELODY CARLSON, author of Diary of a Teenage Girl series and *Torch Red, Color Me Torn*

"Shannon writes with a forthright style, yet she remains tactful and kind as she presents her balanced, godly teaching on dating and relationships. Without question, this is a must-read for any young woman who longs to remain pure in her relationship with God, and I suspect this book will very quickly become a staple of small-group studies."

—FRED STOEKER, coauthor of *Every Young Man's Battle*

"This book should be required reading for any teenage girl who has been exposed to the negative influences of the culture through media, music, movies, and fashion magazines. As someone who is in the trenches of ministry to teen girls, I appreciate Shannon's candid approach and her willingness to tackle some difficult topics facing our young women. She does a beautiful job of exposing the godless issues of the culture while at the same time offering godly solutions."

—VICKI COURTNEY, founder of Virtuous Reality Ministries and author of *Your Girl: Raising a Godly Daughter in an Ungodly World*

"This book is awesome! I will be buying it and reading it with teens that I mentor. I wish it had been available to me when I was a teen."

—ADRIENNE FREAS, homemaker and Campus Crusade for Christ staff member

Shannon Ethridge
& Stephen Arterburn

every young
woman's battle
workbook

How to Pursue Purity in a Sex-Saturated World

WATERBROOK
PRESS

EVERY YOUNG WOMAN'S BATTLE WORKBOOK
PUBLISHED BY WATERBROOK PRESS
2375 Telstar Drive, Suite 160
Colorado Springs, Colorado 80920
A division of Random House, Inc.

ISBN 1-57856-855-2

Published in association with the literary agency of Alive Communications, Inc., 7680 Goddard Street, Suite 200, Colorado Springs, CO 80920.

Printed in the United States of America
2004

10 9 8 7 6 5 4 3 2

contents

foreword

(by Stephen Arterburn)

When Fred Stoeker and I wrote *Every Young Man's Battle,* we began getting e-mails from young guys who said the book really helped them in their struggle for sexual purity. Some fought the battle every day, while others did not even know it was a battle. They thought they were just being "real men" when they viewed pornography or had sex with a girl. We were very grateful for these e-mails.

Then, a few weeks after our book was published, a different kind of e-mail started to arrive. It was from young women who had read the book. Maybe a youth pastor recommended it or they spotted their boyfriend reading it. However they found the book, it seemed to have made an impact. Some said it changed the way they viewed boys and sex. Others literally went through their closets and threw away or gave away clothes that were too revealing and might stir up lust in a young man. And now that they better understood the young men in their lives, they were ready to have their own book about their own struggles. Shannon Ethridge and I wrote *Every Young Woman's Battle* and this workbook in response to those e-mails.

The trends for sexual purity have not been positive over the last few years. In some settings, having sexual intercourse with as many people as possible has become a sport. In others, oral sex is not viewed as real sex but just something you do, like kissing. And in every area the question lingers, "How far is too far?" So the need is obvious for a book like *Every Young*

Woman's Battle, which addresses these issues, as well as for the companion workbook, which offers real-life application. This workbook takes the plainly stated problems and solutions from *Every Young Woman's Battle* and provides a forum for determining practical ways to live a different life—one according to God's standards.

Thank you in advance for trusting us with the time you will spend on both books. When you finish, please e-mail me what you thought of them. We pray and hope they make a difference in your life.

questions you may have about this workbook

What will the *Every Young Woman's Battle Workbook* do for me?

You will gain assurance that *you are not alone.* In fact, a large majority of young people struggle with sexual issues in varying degrees, as you will discover as you go through this workbook. You'll learn to rely on the power of the Holy Spirit to live a life that honors God (and young men) with your thoughts, attitudes, and actions.

As you gain insights into the unique ways young women struggle with sexual and emotional integrity, you'll also discover how to guard not just your body, but also your mind and heart against sexual compromise. Through thought-provoking questions and soul-searching exercises, you'll begin to cherish your sexuality as the beautiful gift of God that it truly is.

Is this workbook enough or do I also need the book *Every Young Woman's Battle?*

Although this workbook contains excerpts from *Every Young Woman's Battle* (each one is marked at the beginning and end by this symbol: 📖), you also need to read the book in order to see the big picture and get the full effect of the concepts presented.

How much time is required? Do I need to work through every part of each chapter?

You should be able to finish each workbook chapter within twenty-five to thirty minutes. Read through each section, spending more time on areas that address your specific needs and less time on those that don't.

Each chapter contains four parts: Planting Good Seeds, Weeding Out Deception, Harvesting Fulfillment, and Growing Together. You can work through the first three sections on your own. They will help you hide God's Word in your heart and recognize things in your life that hinder your ability to win this battle for sexual and emotional integrity. The last section is designed especially for group discussion, although you can also work through it on your own.

How do I organize a small group to go through this workbook?

You'll be amazed at how much more you'll benefit from this book and workbook if you go through it with a group of like-minded young women. If you don't know of an existing group, start one of your own. Whether it's a Sunday school class or youth group, a small group of students at your school, or friends from your neighborhood, invite some girlfriends to look over the book and workbook, and encourage them to invite some of their friends to join the study. Most young women will recognize that there is always room for improvement in the area of sexual and emotional integrity, regardless of whether they have a boyfriend or have had previous sexual experiences.

Set aside about an hour each week (for eight weeks) to read the assigned chapters of the book and to go through the corresponding workbook chapter. Keep your meetings to a reasonable amount of time (approximately sixty to ninety minutes). You want this study to be a blessing—not a burden! If you can't meet evenings or weekends, consider a sack-lunch discussion or meeting in the afternoon.

When young women gather to discuss such an intimate topic, the temptation to rabbit trail with a variety of other, safer topics can be overwhelming, especially for someone who is uncomfortable at first. So designate one person as the group facilitator to ensure the conversation stays on track. This person has no responsibilities to teach, lecture, or prepare anything in advance, but is simply responsible to begin and end the meeting at the agreed times and to move the conversation along in a productive manner.

If being honest with a group of other young women evokes feelings of fear and mistrust in you, turn to Myth 7 in chapter 4 of *Every Young Woman's Battle.* You are truly not alone in your struggles, and other young women need to know they are not alone either. Will you be the one to tell them?

You never know, perhaps your group will prevent or even rescue someone from engaging in destructive sexual experiences. Your accountability group could truly be a lifeline not just for you, but for every young woman who participates.

Whether you are just entering puberty and new to this struggle or an experienced young adult, you can design a rock-solid defense to avoid becoming a casualty of this war. Whether you are sexually pure, hanging on to your virginity by a thread, or sleeping with a guy, you can maintain and/or reclaim your sexual integrity not just throughout your youth, but throughout your whole life. Recognizing and understanding what kind of things can cause every woman, regardless of her age or marital status, to stumble and fall into sexual temptation is the key. By learning to guard your mind, heart, and body against sexual compromise and understanding God's plan for your sexual and emotional fulfillment, you can maneuver your way through your teenage years with grace…and without regrets.

—from chapter 1 of *Every Young Woman's Battle*

Myth 7 - pg. 38

understanding our battle

Read chapters 1–2 of *Every Young Woman's Battle*

🪴 PLANTING GOOD SEEDS
(Personally Seeking God's Truth)

As you consider Jesus' standard of sexual integrity, plant this good seed in your heart:

> Among you there must not be even a hint of sexual
> immorality. (Ephesians 5:3)

1. What do you think "even a hint" means?

As you seek to know God's truth about the abundant life He has for us, plant John 8:31-32 in your heart:

If you hold to my teaching, you are really my disciples. Then
you will know the truth, and the truth will set you free.

2. Is it possible to be a true disciple of Jesus, yet choose not to familiarize
yourself with His teachings or ignore them as if they do not apply to
you? Why or why not?

3. How can followers of Christ know the truth about their sexuality and
sexual integrity?

4. How can understanding and embracing God's truth about sexual integrity set you free? What does this freedom look like? How will you
know you are free?

🗝 WEEDING OUT DECEPTION
(Recognizing the Truth)

> 📖 You don't have to be messed up or even come from a messed-up family to make irresponsible decisions that will mess up your life. Not even "good Christian girls" are exempt from sexual temptations. Not even you. 📖

5. Have you ever told yourself that you would never give in to sexual temptation? Why or why not?

6. Has your perception of who can be affected by sexual temptations changed as a result of reading these first two chapters? If so, how?

7. Of the twenty questions listed in the first chapter, which ones convicted you most? Why?

8. As a result of this conviction, what do you intend to change in order to guard your mind, heart, and body more completely from sexual compromise?

🌾 HARVESTING FULFILLMENT
(Applying the Truth)

📖 Part of God's perfect plan is that we are so physically, mentally, emotionally, and spiritually drawn to the opposite sex that we long for closeness with each other—not just an "I want to sit beside you" closeness, but a deep desire to be intimately connected.

Intimacy can best be defined by breaking the word into its syllables: "in-to-me-see." The longing for connection with the opposite sex is a longing to be seen and accepted for who we really are deep down inside, as well as to see the other person deep inside so that we truly know each other. As a matter of fact, according to Webster's dictionary, one of the definitions of the word *know* is "to have sexual inter-course with."

God designed the male and female bodies so that the penis fits perfectly inside the vagina during the act of sexual intercourse. But sexual intercourse was not intended to be just a *physical* connection. God designed sexual intercourse to be shared between two bodies, two minds, two hearts, and two spirits that unite to become a one-flesh union. When this level of intimacy is experienced within the commitment and safety of a loving marriage, it can be one of the most earthshaking and fulfilling experiences you'll ever know this side of heaven. 📖

9. If God designed sex to be such a powerful bonding experience between a husband and a wife, why do you think so many young people give in to sexual temptations before marriage? What might they be looking for? Do they find it?

10. Do you feel that an intimate one-flesh union between you and your husband-to-be is worth the wait? What consequences do you risk if you don't wait until marriage? What consequences do you risk if you wait? Which is more desirable to you?

❧ GROWING TOGETHER

(Sharing the Truth in Small-Group Discussion)

📖 If you have been successful in overcoming temptations thus far, praise God for His protection, and prepare for further victory. If you have given in to any of these temptations, if you wonder why you feel so disconnected from God, or if you feel anxious about your present or future relationships, this book could be your pathway to peace. 📖

11. What do you hope to gain or learn from studying *Every Young Woman's Battle* and this workbook?

12. How, specifically, can other members of the group encourage you to get everything you hope to gain from this study?

13. What point in the first two chapters most convicted, challenged, or relieved you? Why?

📖 So while young men are primarily aroused by what they see with their eyes, as a young woman you are more aroused by what you hear and feel. The temptation to look at pornography can be overwhelming to a guy, but you may be more likely to read a romance novel or go gaga over a rock star. A male may fantasize about watching a woman undress, but you would be more likely to fantasize about a guy whispering sweet nothings in your ear while touching you gently. A male wants to look and touch, while you would prefer to relate and connect emotionally.

While a guy gets tempted sexually because of what he sees, you are more likely to be tempted sexually because your heart is crying out for someone to satisfy your innermost desire to be loved, needed, valued, and cherished. While a guy also needs mental, emotional, and spiritual connection, his physical needs tend to be in the driver's seat and his other needs ride along in the back. The reverse is true for you. A young woman's emotions are usually in the driver's seat. That's why it's said that guys *give love to get sex* and girls *give sex to get love*. Sadly, we know of many girls who had sex when all they really wanted was someone to hold them. We want you to know that sex outside of marriage will never bring you the love and acceptance you want, but with God's help you can find fulfillment and satisfaction in healthy ways. 📖

14. What differences between guys and girls (chapter 2) most surprised you? How do you feel about those differences?

📖 Sometimes the truth hurts, and it's much easier if we can keep it hidden. As a matter of fact, sometimes the secrets we harbor are so painful that we don't want to face them ourselves. We assume that these secrets will go away if we don't think or talk about them with anyone. But the opposite is true. Shameful secrets fester like a splinter in a finger, and it's much better to name the secret and to let someone help us remove it from our lives so the wound will heal. 📖

15. Do you have any sexual secrets that are doing you more harm than good because you are keeping them to yourself? If you can share them with the group, do so. If you are currently unable to share them with the group for whatever reason, explain the emotions behind your decision not to talk about them (fear, distrust, shame, and so on).

16. How would it make you feel to discover that other girls in the group are struggling with the same issues and emotions that you are currently experiencing?

17. How, specifically, can the group pray for you? What issues would you like help in overcoming? What negative emotions surrounding any unspoken issues would you like to overcome (fear, distrust, shame, and so on)?

✇

*D*ear God, give us the courage to dare to be truthful with ourselves, with You, and with one another. Remind us of Your perfect blueprints for our sexuality, and help us to understand and embrace Your truths that will set us free to live a life of sexual integrity and fulfillment in marriage someday. In Jesus' name. Amen.

building lives of sexual integrity

Read chapters 3–4 of *Every Young Woman's Battle*

🪴 PLANTING GOOD SEEDS

(Personally Seeking God's Truth)

As you search your life for signs of compromise, plant these good seeds in your heart:

> "Everything is permissible"—but not everything is beneficial. "Everything is permissible"—but not everything is constructive. Nobody should seek his own good, but the good of others. (1 Corinthians 10:23-24)

> Jesus said to his disciples: "Things that cause people to sin are bound to come, but woe to that person through whom they come. It would be better for [her] to be thrown into the sea with a millstone tied around [her] neck than for [her] to cause [another] to sin." (Luke 17:1-2)

1. Based on what you read in chapters 3 and 4, what kinds of things may be "permissible" but not necessarily "beneficial" or "constructive" for a young woman to do or say in the presence of the opposite sex? Why are they not "beneficial" or "constructive"?

2. How, specifically, can living a life of sexual integrity help you seek "the good of others" and avoid causing others to sin?

As you seek to rid your life of compromise and build a life of sexual integrity, plant Matthew 7:24-27 in your heart:

> Therefore everyone who hears these words of mine and puts
> them into practice is like a wise man who built his house on
> the rock. The rain came down, the streams rose, and the
> winds blew and beat against that house; yet it did not fall,
> because it had its foundation on the rock. But everyone who
> hears these words of mine and does not put them into prac-
> tice is like a foolish man who built his house on sand. The
> rain came down, the streams rose, and the winds blew and
> beat against that house, and it fell with a great crash.

3. Rewrite this passage of Scripture so that it's about a young woman who is building a life of sexual integrity rather than a house. As you do so, consider the kinds of sexual temptations that will come against her and what will happen if she puts God's words into practice. Consider also what will happen if she fails to put God's words into practice. We've written the first line to get you started.

Therefore everyone who hears these words of mine and puts them into practice is like a wise young woman who builds a life of sexual integrity.

_____

_____

_____

_____

_____

⚒ WEEDING OUT DECEPTION
(Recognizing the Truth)

📖 Unfortunately, the panty line is exactly where too many young women envision sexual integrity to stop and compromise to start. But is the panty line really where compromise begins? 📖

4. Can a young woman avoid going past the panty line, yet still have sexual compromise in her life? Why or why not?

5. Where do you think the line between sexual compromise and integrity lies? How would you explain this to a friend?

📖 But it's no laughing matter when one of the legs of your sexuality buckles, because then your life can become a slippery slope leading to discontentment, sexual compromise, self-loathing, and emotional brokenness. When this happens, God's blessing, intended to bring richness and pleasure to your life, feels more like a curse that brings great pain and despair.

As we mentioned, your sexuality is comprised of four distinct aspects: the physical, mental, emotional, and spiritual dimensions of your being. These four parts combine to form the unique individual God designed you to be. Again, your sexuality isn't *what you do.* Your sexuality is *who you are,* and you are made with a body, mind, heart, and spirit, not just a body. So, sexual integrity is not just about remaining physically abstinent. It is about purity in all four aspects of your being—body, mind, heart, and spirit. When all four aspects line up perfectly, your "tabletop" (your sexuality) reflects balance and integrity. 📖

6. Is your life a slippery slope or a life of balance and integrity? Which legs of your sexuality, if any, are broken? How can these areas of your life be repaired and strengthened?

7. What benefits will be yours as a result of guarding your body, mind, heart, and spirit from compromise? What concerns will you not have to worry about? What kind of things can you look forward to?

HARVESTING FULFILLMENT
(Applying the Truth)

📖 If you think being a person of sexual integrity means that you are a boring, frigid young woman who never has any fun with a guy, nothing can be further from the truth. A young woman of sexual integrity is free to enjoy the excitement and fun of a romantic relationship without all the worry that compromise brings into our lives.

Compromise is the opposite of integrity. It leads you to do things that take your mind and heart away from Christ. It usually begins in small ways but eventually blossoms into big-time sin that controls you.

So if you want to live a life of sexual integrity, you will be undivided in your devotion to sexual purity, refusing to be controlled by your sexual passions. When you exercise self-control, you will be free to share yourself completely with your husband in a passionate sexual relationship without the scars and emotional baggage that can come with compromise. Just think how much your husband will love that you saved your sexual pleasures especially for him and that you can love him with reckless abandon, not just with your body, but also your mind, heart, and soul. 📖

8. Have you been under the impression that acting with complete integrity would make you a boring girl who doesn't have any fun? If so, how has your perception changed since reading this book?

9. How, specifically, can exercising self-control help you enjoy your current life more fully? How might it affect your future?

✿ GROWING TOGETHER

(Sharing the Truth in Small-Group Discussion)

10. What insights have you gained from this study so far? Why are they valuable to you and how can they serve you in life?

11. What myths in chapter 4 have you believed in the past? Beside each, write what truth dispels this myth.

📖 Let's put this all together. If you want to be a young woman of sexual and emotional integrity, make sure that your thoughts, words, emotions, and actions reflect an inner beauty and a sincere love for God, others, and yourself. Not that you will never be tempted to think, say, feel, or do something inappropriate, but you will try diligently to resist these temptations and stand firm in your convictions. You won't use the opposite sex in an attempt to get your emotional cravings met, nor will you entertain sexual fantasies. You won't dress to seek male attention, but you won't limit your wardrobe to ankle-length skirts and turtleneck sweaters, either. You'll dress fashionably and look sharp and maybe even appear sexy to a guy (like beauty, "sexy" is in the eye of the beholder, and some guys will think you look sexy even when you dress modestly), but your motivation won't be self-seeking or seductive. You will present yourself as an attractive young woman because you know you represent God to others.

Your life will line up with your lip. If you claim to be a follower of Christ, you won't disregard His many teachings on sexual immorality, lustful thoughts, immodest dress, and inappropriate talk. You will live what you believe about God, and your beauty will shine from the inside out. Finally, you will have an incredible hope for your future marriage—that it will be everything God intended for it to be, especially the passionate sexual relationship you and your husband will be able to enjoy. 📖

12. What do you consider to be the biggest challenges young women face in the battle for sexual integrity? Why?

13. What is the best advice you can give to someone struggling to overcome those challenges?

    📖 It's our hope that if you know how common these issues are to young women, you won't hesitate to discuss your own sexual struggles with a trusted adult or a mature Christian girlfriend. We believe that 99.9 percent of all women face sexual temptations in varying degrees.

Paul tells us in 1 Corinthians 10:13: "No temptation has seized you except what is common to [woman]. And God is faithful; he will not let you be tempted beyond what you can bear. But when you are tempted, he will also provide a way out so that you can stand up under it." Paul didn't say, "If you experience sexual temptation, there must be something wrong with you because no one else struggles with it that much." He said that all temptations are "common." And because God creates all human beings (regardless of gender, nationality, or economic background) as sexual human beings, you can bet that sexual and relational temptations are by far the most common temptations on the planet. 📖

14. Prior to this study, did you ever feel as if you were the *only one* who struggled with a particular sexual issue? If so, why do you think you felt this way?

15. How does it make you feel to know how common these issues are?

16. Does it make you willing to be more open about your personal struggles? Why or why not?

17. Does it make you more open to listening to and supporting other young women in their struggles? Why or why not?

∞

Lord Jesus, help us as we attempt to build lives of sexual integrity and become the strong women You created us to be. Dispel the myths in our minds that we are the only ones who struggle with sexual issues, and give us the courage and confidence to boldly approach You so that we may receive Your help when we need it. Help us encourage and support one another as we take off our masks and get real with one another. Teach us to love one another unconditionally, as You have loved us. Amen.

avoiding self-destruction

Read chapters 5–8 in *Every Young Woman's Battle*.

PLANTING GOOD SEEDS
(Personally Seeking God's Truth)

As you seek victory in the battle for sexual and emotional integrity, plant this good seed in your heart:

> Dear friends, I urge you, as aliens and strangers in the world,
> to abstain from sinful desires, which war against your soul.
> (1 Peter 2:11)

1. Do you agree that you have desired things that are destructive to you? Explain your answer as it relates to the material in this section.

2. What "sinful desires" do you abstain from? How can this choice help you win the battle for sexual and emotional integrity?

As you seek genuine, lasting beauty, plant these seeds in your heart:

Charm is deceptive, and beauty is fleeting;
  but a woman who fears [respects and serves] the Lord
    is to be praised.
    ✳ (Proverbs 31:30)

For you created my inmost being;
  You knit me together in my mother's womb.
I praise you because I am fearfully and wonderfully made;
  your works are wonderful,
    I know that full well.
My frame was not hidden from you
  when I was made in the secret place.
When I was woven together in the depths of the earth,
  your eyes saw my unformed body.
All the days ordained for me
  were written in your book
    before one of them came to be.
    ✳ (Psalm 139:13-16)

3. Do you know, beyond a shadow of a doubt, that you are "fearfully and wonderfully made"? Can you wholeheartedly thank God for His handiwork when you look in the mirror? Why or why not?

⚓ WEEDING OUT DECEPTION
(Recognizing the Truth)

📖 The momentary relief that self-gratification may provide is not worth the long-term stress it can create. It can lead to shame, low self-esteem, and fear of what others might think or that something is wrong with you....

We also believe that masturbation is not healthy because it can train a person to "fly solo," to operate independently of anyone else. When you masturbate, you train your body as well as your mind what to find pleasurable and how to orgasm. When you marry, if your husband isn't able to please you in the exact same way, this could make your marital sex life very frustrating and disappointing. 📖

4. Which of the arguments against masturbation discussed in chapter 5 do you feel are convincing reasons for you to refrain from it? (Check all that apply.)

___ Masturbation often involves sexual fantasies about people you are not married to, which the Bible says is sin.

___ It can lead to greater sexual temptations as you fuel your own sexual fires.

___ Masturbation can become habit-forming and addicting.

___ It often leads to shame, low self-esteem, and fear of what others may think.

___ Self-gratification assumes that God can't help you control your sexual desires.

___ Habitual masturbation can cause you to feel distanced from God.

___ It can train your body to "fly solo."

5. What did you learn about masturbation from reading chapter 5? What is your personal choice regarding masturbation? Why?

📖 While rape and sexual abuse are absolute tragedies, the tragedy deepens if the abused person doesn't get help for coping with the rape or abuse. When the wounds of abuse go untreated, the abused person often becomes an abuser of others....

Remember, you are a child of God, the bride of Christ, and a precious daughter of the King of the universe. Even if someone treats you less than royally or uses you for a purpose other than what God intended, *never forget who you really are.*

You deserve to be treated with dignity and respect. Period.

Also remember that others are worthy of the same respect. Don't allow the cycle of abuse to continue to destroy your life and your relationships. Draw a line in the sand and refuse to allow your future to be hindered by your past. God has great things in store for you as you seek to discover the true purpose for which you were created—a divine purpose, indeed! 📖

6. If you have been abused by someone in any way, which of the following have you been tempted to do? (Check all that apply.)

___ suffer in silence, assuming no one would believe you or understand

___ put up with the abuse because you felt desperate to have that person in your life

___ believe that you did something to deserve the abuse

___ take out your anger for your abuser on other people in your life

___ assume that you are no longer sexually pure or valuable as a person

___ harbor bitterness and resentment against your abuser

___ allow the burden you are carrying to weigh you down

7. What, specifically, can you do to pursue healing from past abuse? Who are some people you could talk to about what you have gone through? If you have not experienced abuse, who could you talk to if you ever sense that someone is trying to sexually abuse you?

8. How can you know that you are in danger of abusing someone else?
✳ How can a person break the cycle of abuse?

9. How have you experienced God's help in overcoming tragedy? In what way could you use your testimony of triumph to encourage others in their healing from abuse?

🐚 HARVESTING FULFILLMENT
(Applying the Truth)

📖 We hope you like what you see in the mirror because you are one of God's beautiful creations, but we also hope that you don't let your beauty go to your head. Somewhere in between "I hate the way I look!" and "Look at me! Aren't I hot?" lies a delicate balance that we pray you will find and maintain throughout life. Why is this so important? Because either extreme can lead you down the path of sexual compromise at lightning speed. 📖

10. Have you experienced either extreme—having an incredibly poor self-image or an overinflated self-image? If so, how did it affect your life or your relational pursuits?

11. How, specifically, can you maintain a healthy balance between a poor self-image and an overinflated one? What will the result be if you can maintain this balance throughout life?

📖 Internet relationships can be misleading and harmful to your ability to form healthy relationships with guys you interact with in person. It is hard for any real relationship to live up to the fantasy of a virtual relationship....

Also, in virtual relationships you get only a one-dimensional view of someone's character. You see only the side that the person allows you to see. However, in real relationships, you get a more complex, three-dimensional view as you watch how a guy interacts with his parents, how he treats his little sister, how he treats his friends as well as other girls, and so on. You need to see all of these things before you can make a fair judgment about a person's true character and whether he is appealing to you or not....

You may have heard some people say that fantasy relationships are much better than real ones, but is this true? Not by
a long shot. Perhaps people who pursue virtual relationships
have never tasted how good reality can be. When someone
knows you inside and out, knows all your little quirks and
annoying habits, knows everything about you there is to
know, and yet is absolutely crazy about you, it's an awesome
thing. Such genuine intimacy enhances your self-esteem,
your life, and your happiness. 📖

12. Have you ever been under the impression that you could develop an
intimate relationship with a stranger over the Internet? If so, has this
book changed your perception? Why or why not?

13. Do you prefer real or virtual relationships? Why?

14. What benefits do real relationships offer that Internet relationship
cannot? Explain your answer.

15. If a friend becomes involved in a cyber-relationship, how could you help her understand that she really can't know this person unless he is a part of her world and she a part of his?

🌿 GROWING TOGETHER
(Sharing the Truth in Small-Group Discussion)

16. Which parts of these chapters meant the most to you? If you feel safe doing so, explain why by identifying the helpful insights you gained.

17. Whether or not the issues have been a problem for you, what are some practical things you can do to avoid self-destruction in any of these areas?

📖 We thought about inserting a graph or chart in this chapter to show minimum and maximum weights for young women, but decided against it. Why? Because we don't want to perpetuate the myth that your beauty comes from a particular number on your bathroom scales. Yet, even though true beauty cannot be measured by outward appearances, looking good on the outside is relatively important because you represent God. The secret to looking and feeling your personal best is eating healthy foods and exercising your body. As you simply eat the right foods in the right amounts and exercise to enhance or maintain your metabolism and muscle strength, your body will settle into a weight that is absolutely perfect for you.

But your beauty is not "on hold" until you reach a perfect weight. You can feel beautiful at any weight, or you can be miserable until your scale reads some magical number that you may never reach or be satisfied with. The choice is yours. 📖

18. Do you frequently look for affirmation about your physical appearance from others? from the bathroom scale? from guys? Explain your answer.

19. How can you "choose" beauty today, regardless of your weight or the condition of your hair, skin, nails, and so on?

      📖 What about you? What do you want to be remembered for? Your obsession with your own appearance and weight or your passion to love and serve others? Do you want to spend your life looking into mirrors, distracted by your own reflection and how your looks compare to others, or do you want to invest your life looking beyond yourself and into a world of people who need to experience the love of God through you? 📖

20. In the space below, write a brief summary of what you want people to say about you at the end of your life. If it would help, imagine you are at your own funeral and write the summary as a eulogy. Share your summary with the group.

21. Based on your life today and the choices you are making, how close are you to being the person you want others to remember? What changes do you need to make in order to line up your life with this goal?

⧈

Heavenly Father, help us avoid self-destructive behaviors, such as masturbation, and go to You for healing if our self-image is poor or overinflated. Give us the strength to avoid unhealthy virtual relationships and to break the cycle of abuse. Remind us that You can satisfy us completely and that we are beautiful simply because You made us. Help us to continue being real with people, treating others with the dignity and respect they deserve. Show us Your perfect plan for our lives and help us follow it without hesitation. In Jesus' name. Amen.

avoiding the destruction of others

Read chapters 9–11 in *Every Young Woman's Battle*.

 PLANTING GOOD SEEDS
(Personally Seeking God's Truth)

As you seek to use your power in healthy, God-honoring ways, plant 2 Corinthians 10:3-5 (MSG) in your heart:

> The world doesn't fight fair. But we don't live or fight our
> battles that way.... The tools of our trade aren't for market-
> ing or manipulation, but they are for demolishing that entire
> massively corrupt culture. We use our powerful God-tools
> for smashing warped philosophies, tearing down barriers
> erected against the truth of God, fitting every loose thought
> and emotion and impulse into the structure of life shaped by
> Christ. Our tools are ready at hand for clearing the ground
> of every obstruction and building lives of obedience into
> maturity.

1. How do you see young women misusing their power? How does this scripture say we should use power?

As you think about how a young woman of sexual integrity should clothe herself, plant these good seeds in your heart:

> Rather, clothe yourselves with the Lord Jesus Christ, and
> do not think about how to gratify the desires of the sinful
> nature. (Romans 13:14)

> She is clothed with strength and dignity;
> she can laugh at the days to come.
> (Proverbs 31:25)

2. What do you think it means to "clothe" yourself with Christ? with strength? with dignity? How could such clothing help you resist sexual temptation and "laugh at the days to come"?

As you consider the incredible power of your words and your actions, plant these good seeds in your heart:

> Even a child is known by [her] actions,
> by whether [her] conduct is pure and right.
> (Proverbs 20:11)

> Words from a wise [woman's] mouth are gracious,
>> but a fool is consumed by [her] own lips.
> At the beginning [her] words are folly;
>> at the end they are wicked madness.
>> (Ecclesiastes 10:12-13)

> [She] who loves a pure heart and whose speech is gracious
>> will have the king for [her] friend.
>> (Proverbs 22:11)

3. How can your words and actions bring destruction into your life? into the lives of others?

4. How can your words and actions bring peace and power into your life? into the lives of others?

WEEDING OUT DECEPTION
(Recognizing the Truth)

📖 Many young women think that because they are "only flirting," they're not hurting anyone. But is this true? Is flirting always an innocent, fun game?…

Even though Alicia, Rachel, and Diana were just "having fun," their flirting led these guys to believe they were interested in a romantic or physical relationship with them—and the guys acted on that belief. (Duh!) Even though they had intentionally tried to make these guys' eyes pop out of their heads with seductive remarks and behaviors, they also intended for the guys to look but not touch. Do you see why certain kinds of flirting are cruel to a guy—and cruel for him to do to you? 📖

5. Describe the difference between being friendly with a guy and flirting with him.

6. Why do you think young women flirt with guys? What do they think they'll gain from such behavior?

7. What effect can flirting have on the young man being toyed with? on the young woman doing the flirting? Does any good come of flirting? Why or why not?

🦬 HARVESTING FULFILLMENT
(Applying the Truth)

📖 Let us provide some balance to this discussion. We're not asking you to become powerless and lay down your rights for any guy so he can walk all over you, sexually or otherwise. Everyone needs a sense of personal power. It's healthy and appropriate to use that power to guard yourself from guys who are seeking to control or coerce you through verbal, physical, or sexual abuse or are insisting that you "put out" for them sexually. Use your power to guard yourself against being taken advantage of and mistreated. But don't use your power to take advantage of others and mistreat them. Do unto others as you would have them do unto you (see Matthew 7:12). Respect others and expect them to respect you. 📖

8. What are some healthy ways you have used your power in your relationships with guys?

9. What are some unhealthy ways?

10. Have you ever chosen to give up all your rights by allowing a guy to persuade you to do things physically that made you feel uncomfortable or that you didn't want to do? If so, why do you think you allowed yourself to be used? What can you do to ensure that you don't allow yourself to be mistreated or abused again?

11. How can you strike a healthy balance between overpowering a guy (being manipulative or demanding) and being overpowered by him (allowing him to use and abuse you)? Describe in your own words what it means to respect others and to expect them to respect you.

❧ GROWING TOGETHER

(Sharing the Truth in Small-Group Discussion)

12. What did you learn from these chapters that you didn't know before? What are some areas that you may need to change if you are going to win the battle for sexual and emotional integrity?

13. What practical things can you do to make changes in these areas?

📖 We are living in an age when many women are using guys for their own self-satisfaction and are more predatory than their male counterparts. Many are desperate for affirmation that they are desirable and often control others in their pursuit of that affirmation. While it's appropriate and healthy for any female not to want to be overpowered by a male, it's not appropriate to strive for the reverse—*girls overpowering guys.* 📖

14. Do you agree that many young women have become more sexually predatory than young men? Why or why not? What evidence do you see of this?

15. What is the payoff or reward that a young woman seeks in bringing a man to his knees with her charms? Does this tactic usually work or does it backfire on her? How so?

📖 As a matter of fact, youth pastors tell us, "I'm stunned by how the girls walk into youth group wearing totally immodest clothes! Don't they know they're in church? Don't they know that boys are visually stimulated? Don't they know they give people the wrong impression when they dress seductively for attention?" Unfortunately, too many young women *don't* realize these things, or if they do, they are so desperate for attention (even if it's unhealthy attention) that they ignore wisdom.

But if you want to be a young woman of sexual integrity, you will be different. Smarter. You will teach your guy friends how to treat you with dignity and respect rather than teaching them that you are eye candy or a toy for their sexual jollies. When you catch a young man's eye, it will be because of the way you carry yourself with confidence and character, not because of your skimpy attire. The guy whose head you turn with your inward beauty will more than likely be a godly young man who could possibly make a great husband someday, not some Joe Schmoe who just wants to use your body for his temporary pleasure. You will look to God's Word to determine how you dress, and be an example of purity and modesty for your generation. 📖

16. When you evaluated the clothes hanging in your closet, did you find any questionable items? What were they and why were they questionable? What adjustments, if any, can you make to your wardrobe to ensure modesty?

17. Are you willing to invite the girls in your small group to confront you privately if they ever see you wearing something that isn't modest? Are you willing to do the same for them? Explain your answer.

Question 20

18. What does a young woman hope to gain by wearing immodest or seductive clothes? Does she actually gain what she wants with such attire? Why or why not?

19. How can you set a high standard and be an example of purity and modesty for your generation? Is such a goal something you are interested in accomplishing? Why or why not?

20. What are some practical, nonoffensive things you could say to help a friend who dresses immodestly?

∞

Lord, help us to be good stewards of the power You give us as attractive young women. Show us how to be examples of modesty and purity in how we dress. Teach us how to guard our mouths and to use our words wisely to build others up rather than to tear them down or tempt them sexually. Give us a genuine love and appreciation for others and help us to respect young men and earn their respect as well. In Jesus' most holy and precious name. Amen.

guarding your mind

Read chapters 12–14 in *Every Young Woman's Battle*.

🪴 PLANTING GOOD SEEDS
(Personally Seeking God's Truth)

As you seek God's mercy and grace, plant Hebrews 4:15-16 in your heart:

> For we do not have a high priest who is unable to sympa-
> thize with our weaknesses, but we have one who has been
> tempted in every way, just as we are—yet was without sin.
> Let us then approach the throne of grace with confidence,
> so that we may receive mercy and find grace to help us in
> our time of need.

1. How does it make you feel to know that Jesus understands what it's
   like to be tempted and that you can approach Him with confidence?

As you seek to have pure thoughts and guard your mind, plant these good seeds in your heart:

> Therefore, I urge you, [sisters], in view of God's mercy, to offer your bodies as living sacrifices, holy and pleasing to God—this is your spiritual act of worship. Do not conform any longer to the pattern of this world, but be transformed by the renewing of your mind. Then you will be able to test and approve what God's will is—his good, pleasing and perfect will. (Romans 12:1-2)

> Whatever is true, whatever is noble, whatever is right, whatever is pure, whatever is lovely, whatever is admirable—if anything is excellent or praiseworthy—think about such things. (Philippians 4:8)

2. What do you think it means not to conform to the "pattern of this world"? What does it mean to be "transformed by the renewing of your mind"? How can you renew your mind?

As you seek to live an open-book life before God, plant Jeremiah 17:10 in your heart:

> I the LORD search the heart
> and examine the mind,
> to reward a [woman] according to [her] conduct,
> according to what [her] deeds deserve.

3. How does this verse inspire us to guard our minds against sexual sin? What rewards do you think the Lord grants to those who try to guard their minds?

✎ WEEDING OUT DECEPTION
(Recognizing the Truth)

> 📖 I learned the hard way that when you fill your mind with sexual images [from media], you awaken sexual desires that should only be entertained and fulfilled within marriage....
>
> If you have a steady diet of messages in the media that weaken your defenses in the battle for sexual integrity, we strongly urge you to go on a starvation diet. When you starve your appetite for sin, it loses its power over you. Then your hunger for righteousness and purity begin driving your thoughts, actions, and attitudes. 📖

4. Do you need to go on a starvation diet from a particular form of media? Explain your answer.

5. What will change if you go on such a starvation diet? What will happen if instead you continue to feed these media monsters? Which result do you prefer? Why?

    📖 As a society, we have become so desensitized to sexual messages that we often unscrew our heads, put them under the La-Z-Boy recliner, and allow the television and other forms of media to fill our minds with worldly scripts. 📖

6. Make a list of all the types of media you enjoy. Include specific magazines, books, movies, television shows, music, and Web sites.

7. Now follow the directions on pages 128–129 of *Every Young Woman's Battle* about how to "master the media." Which of the previously mentioned forms of media should you consider eliminating? Explain your answer.

8. What makes these forms of media so appealing to you? Is their entertainment value worth compromising your sexual integrity? Why or why not?

📖 HARVESTING FULFILLMENT
(Applying the Truth)

> 📖 Sow a thought, reap an action;
> Sow an action, reap a habit;
> Sow a habit, reap a character;
> Sow a character, reap a destiny.
> —Samuel Smiles 📖

9. Answer each of the following questions with one or two descriptive phrases.

What kind of destiny do you hope to have?

What kind of character is necessary for such a destiny?

What kinds of habits are necessary for such a character?

What kinds of actions are necessary for such habits?

What kinds of thoughts are necessary for such actions?

10. How would you characterize your current thought life? What impact will it have on your destiny?

📖 Have you ever tried to stop doing something that you knew was wrong but just couldn't stop? Ever tried to be more disciplined in a certain area of your life, only to cave under pressure?

These battles are fairly predictable. When both good and evil battle within you, do you know who will eventually take the prize? When your flesh wrestles with your spirit, do you know who will eventually win? *Whichever one you feed the most.* If you feast on MTV and romance novels, you can bet that your flesh takes control when you face sexual temptations. However, if you feast on God's Word, prayer, and healthy relationships with godly people, your spirit can consistently overpower your flesh, even in the midst of fierce temptations. 📖

11. Use your own words to describe how feasting on sex-saturated forms of media affects your ability to overcome sexual temptations.

12. How would feasting on mental images which support Christian sexual values help you win the battle for sexual integrity? What are some practical ways to do this?

❧ GROWING TOGETHER
(Sharing the Truth in Small-Group Discussion)

13. Share with the group some of the insights you have gained about your media habits. Are there particular shows, musicians, magazines, and so on that you've chosen to give up for the sake of mastering the media? Explain your answer.

14. Which particular forms of entertainment can you feel good about? Why?

    📖 How would you feel if every guy you encountered had the ability to read your mind, just by being in your presence? Does that possibility make you nervous?…

    And what if every female developed this ability too?…

    Even though you can rest assured that others aren't likely to develop this ability anytime soon, you have an even bigger concern. God has had it all along.

    What's on the inside of your heart and mind? Could you, like David, be so bold as to pray such a thing as this: "Test me, O LORD, and try me, examine my heart and my mind" (Psalm 26:2)? Notice David didn't say, "Examine my actions." He asked God to examine what he was *thinking*. 📖

15. How would you feel if others were aware of every inappropriate thought that goes through your mind? Why? What does your answer tell you?

📖 While we don't know of anyone who intentionally be-comes addicted to pornography, we have met young people who innocently stumbled onto a pornographic movie or Web site....

It's also disturbing how pornography can suddenly land right in front of your eyes, even when you are not looking for it....

Pornography can be addicting and consume your mind with thoughts that continue to plague you, even when your eyes are closed. 📖

16. When has pornography just seemed to jump out at you from nowhere? What did you do?

17. What will you do if your eyes come across something pornographic again?

📖 To help answer the question about what effect your thoughts have on you, imagine an actor preparing to perform in a play. She memorizes her lines, gets inside the character's head, and tries to understand how this person would feel and act. She rehearses being that person. She thinks intently about doing what that person would do and saying what that person would say, exactly the way she would say it. The more she's rehearsed being that character, the sharper and more "automatic" her performance.

Something similar happens when you fantasize about sexually or emotionally inappropriate behavior. You are rehearsing when you imagine the conversations you would have with someone if you were ever alone with that individual. You are rehearsing when you envision a sexually intimate encounter. You are rehearsing when you envision what you'll say and do in these encounters. Rehearsing makes you susceptible to acting out the scenarios you have been fantasizing about. It feeds your desire and breaks down your resistance. So when Satan lays the trap and presents you with a similar compromising situation, guess what? More than likely you will play the part exactly the way you have rehearsed it. If you don't guard your mind, you'll find that when it comes to your relationships with the opposite sex, your resistance can be low before any encounter takes place. 📖

18. Practice getting inside the head of a young woman of sexual and emotional integrity. Imagine what she would be thinking and how she would respond to certain temptations. Then break into pairs and role-play each of the following situations.

A friend wants to watch an R-rated movie that you know has graphic sexual scenes. *What will you do?*

A handsome guy you've been seeing for a while suggests that the two of you move to a more "physical level" in your relationship, putting pressure on you to perform sexually. *How will you respond?*

A well-meaning relative offers you a ticket to a Britney Spears concert. *What's the best course of action?*

∞

*L*ord, help us play the role of a young woman of sexual integrity with grace and style. Help us to guard our minds against media monsters that lead us into temptation. Teach us to be selective about what we allow to come into our minds, and help us focus on things that are pleasing to You. Thank You for giving us the mind of Christ and a divine destiny. Amen.

guarding your heart

Read chapters 15–18 in *Every Young Woman's Battle*.

 PLANTING GOOD SEEDS
(Personally Seeking God's Truth)

As you seek to guard your heart against unhealthy relationships, plant Proverbs 4:23 in your heart:

> Above all else, guard your heart,
>   for it is the wellspring of life.

1. What does this verse mean to you personally?

In order to better understand God's view of sexual and emotional compromise, plant this good seed in your heart:

You know the next commandment pretty well, too: "Don't go to bed with another's spouse." But don't think you've preserved your virtue simply by staying out of bed. Your heart can be corrupted by lust even quicker than your body. Those leering looks [or thoughts] you think nobody notices—they also corrupt. (Matthew 5:27-28, MSG)

2. What does it mean to lust after a guy in your heart?

⚒ WEEDING OUT DECEPTION
(Recognizing the Truth)

📖 Many young women ask us, "Will I ever get to the point that I don't notice cute guys anymore than I notice anyone else?" While your awareness of the opposite sex will likely lessen with time and maturity, it will never go away completely. Remember, the desire for love, attention, affection, and relational connection is part of the human condition. It doesn't change because you graduate from high school, because you put a wedding band on your finger, because you have kids, or because you grow old and develop wrinkles and gray hair. The day you stop desiring those things is the day you die. 📖

3. Have you ever thought that once you had a boyfriend (or husband), you'd never look at another guy again? Is it possible to only have eyes for one person and not even notice any other guy, or do we simply have to guard our eyes from looking outside of committed relationships? Explain your answer.

     📖 Maybe you've locked eyes with a guy and wondered, *Could this be love at first sight?* No, it's not. There's no such thing as love at first sight, only *attention* at first sight. Love isn't an exhilarating feeling, it's a serious commitment that you make after getting to know a person through an extended investment of time and energy. 📖

4. What's the difference between love at first sight and genuine love?

5. If a guy you didn't know approached you and said, "I fell in love with you at first sight!" how would you feel? Would you believe him? How would you respond?

📖 Despite the messages you receive from the media, being attracted to someone doesn't mean you have to do anything about your attraction. If you are attracted to a particular male friend, don't assume you're going to wind up fooling around with him someday and so attempt to sexualize the relationship. You are *not* powerless over your emotions. You are not "destined" to be with him or to have sex with him, as if you could do nothing to stop it. In fact, you can ignore him altogether if you so choose, whether you do so because the age difference is too great or because he doesn't share your interests and values or because something about him makes the relationship forbidden. 📖

6. What would happen if every time you felt drawn to another person you followed through on your feelings? How long could you remain committed to your boyfriend or to your husband if you followed your emotions instead of guarding your heart?

🌾 HARVESTING FULFILLMENT
(Applying the Truth)

📖 Just as a yellow traffic light can quickly turn red, attachments with the wrong person can quickly lead to major relational wrecks!

At this point, in all honesty, love is often blind. You can be so enamored by all the wonderful things you see in him that the bad things fade into the background. That is why it is important to get to know a guy well before you become emotionally attached to him and become a couple. Identify both his strengths and weaknesses before deciding he's a guy you want to commit to and date exclusively. 📖

📖 All relationships are absolutely wonderful in the beginning. Tons of guys can thrill you and delight your heart in the first few weeks or months of a relationship. But only time will tell if his love, respect, and commitment to you are genuine. Do yourself a favor and be patient. Just as a rosebud's beauty would be destroyed if it was forced open prematurely, the true beauty of a relationship can't be forced either. You can't rush a healthy romantic relationship. By its very nature, it requires time to blossom into its full, God-given potential. 📖

7. What are some of the dangers of rushing a relationship? List as many as you can.

8. What are the benefits of allowing a relationship to unfold slowly over time? List as many as you can.

📖 When we emotionally attach ourselves over and over to different people, we can lose our emotional "stickiness." So if you continue to have one boyfriend after another after another simply out of habit, you may compromise your ability to remain committed and faithful to one person for a lifetime. When you go from person to person and indulge in a new "flavor of the month" whenever you get a little bored in a relationship, you set yourself up to always crave something new. Then when you find a good guy and settle down, your old patterns of relating can come back to tempt you. As soon as the new wears off your marriage, the craving to sample yet another flavor can be overwhelming. 📖

9. What can you do now to help ensure that you will be emotionally faithful to your husband someday?

🌿 GROWING TOGETHER

(Sharing the Truth in Small-Group Discussion)

📖 Everyone longs to feel loved, and there's nothing sinful about this desire. The problem lies in where we look for love. If you are not getting the love you need from appropriate places, such as your family or healthy friendships, you may go searching for it with reckless abandon. But God has a better way. You don't have to put your heart and body in jeopardy just because you want to be loved. You can seek loving, healthy relationships *and* guard your heart from compromise at the same time. 📖

10. Have you ever looked for love in any of the wrong places discussed in this section? Where have you looked? What was the result of your pursuit?

📖 Perhaps in the past you have felt that guarding your heart was a gray issue and that it's impossible for a young woman to know how to keep her heart in check. Hopefully, these past few chapters have helped you colorize this issue of emotional integrity with green-, yellow-, and red-light levels so you can identify when you are good to go, when you need to proceed with caution, and when you need to stop altogether before you crash. With this new understanding of emotional integrity, you'll be better able to avoid confusion, false guilt, premature emotional attachment, forbidden relationships, and so on. But best of all, when God sees you are guarding your heart, He will reward you with an even greater revelation of Himself and His extravagant love for you. 📖

11. In your own words, explain the stages of the green-light level of emotional connection and why these are acceptable.

Attention

Attraction

12. Explain the stages of the yellow-light level of emotional connection and why we need to exercise caution with these stages.

Affection

Attachment

13. Finally, explain the stages of the red-light level and why we need to stop before crossing these lines.

Affairs

Addictions

14. How would you explain the concept of guarding your heart to a friend? Get in pairs and practice explaining the green-, yellow-, and red-light levels of emotional connection in such a way that a person who has never read this book would understand.

∞

Dear God, we stand in awe of how you made us to be emotionally stimulated creatures. Thank You for the gifts of attraction and excitement that You give us to enjoy in relationships. Help us to guard our hearts against sexual and emotional compromise so that we can experience the fullness of Your love and the love of our husbands someday without guilt, regret, or emotional baggage. Thank You for cleansing our hearts and teaching us how to be women of sexual and emotional integrity. In Jesus' name. Amen.

guarding your body

Read chapters 19–22 in *Every Young Woman's Battle*.

🥤 PLANTING GOOD SEEDS
(Personally Seeking God's Truth)

As you seek to guard your body against the devastating consequences of sexual sin, plant these seeds in your heart:

> Flee from sexual immorality. All other sins a [woman] commits are outside [her] body, but [she] who sins sexually sins against [her] own body. Do you not know that your body is a temple of the Holy Spirit, who is in you, whom you have received from God? You are not your own; you were bought at a price. Therefore honor God with your body. (1 Corinthians 6:18-20)

> Do not be deceived: God cannot be mocked. A [woman] reaps what [she] sows. The one who sows to please [her] sinful nature, from that nature will reap destruction; the one who sows to please the Spirit, from the Spirit will reap eternal life. (Galatians 6:7-8)

1. What does it mean to "honor God with your body"?

2. What do you think it means to "sow to please the sinful nature"? If you sow these kinds of seeds, what will you reap? Why?

As you seek to understand God's perfect plan for our sexual enjoyment, plant Hebrews 13:4 in your heart:

> Marriage should be honored by all, and the marriage bed kept pure.

3. What do you think it means to honor marriage? How do you think honoring marriage is honoring to God?

4. List as many benefits you can think of that result from avoiding pre-marital or extramarital sex.

⚘ WEEDING OUT DECEPTION
(Recognizing the Truth)

📖 Certain segments of society have convinced many people that if you have protected sex, you won't have to fear disease. While using a condom may make sex more safe than unprotected sex, condoms by no means make sex safe. Dr. Susan Weller says, "It is a disservice to encourage the belief that condoms *will prevent* sexual transmission of HIV."[1] In a study to determine if condoms protect against the spread of HIV, researchers estimate that the true effectiveness of condoms in risk reduction is only 69 percent. With a 31 percent risk factor, using condoms to prevent the spread of HIV is about as dangerous as putting two bullets in a six-chamber gun and playing Russian roulette. Not very smart, huh?

---

1. Susan C. Weller, "A Meta-Analysis of Condom Effectiveness in Reducing Sexually Transmitted HIV," *University of Texas Medical Branch (UTMB) News* (June 7, 1993), *Social Science and Medicine,* 36:36:1635-44.

If you truly want to protect yourself, you'll guard against sexual compromise altogether. No condom fully protects you against the possible physical consequences of sex outside of marriage. No condom protects you against the spiritual consequences of sin, which is broken fellowship with God. No condom will protect you from the emotional consequences of a broken heart. As a matter of fact, studies show that once a teenage girl engages in sexual intercourse outside of marriage, she becomes three times more likely to commit suicide than a girl who is a virgin.[2] When a girl gives her virginity away, it usually results in low self-esteem, regret, shame, and enormous emotional pain. Therefore, don't think in terms of "safe sex," but in terms of "saving sex" until marriage. 📖

5. What would you say to a girlfriend who told you she carries a condom in her purse "just in case"?

6. List as many reasons as you can why condoms are an unwise choice for a young woman who wants to live with sexual integrity.

---

2. Ed Vitagliano, "Study Finds Teen Sex, Suicide Are Linked," *AFA Journal,* October 2003, www .crosswalk.com/family/parenting/teens/1224668.html.

📖 HARVESTING FULFILLMENT

(Applying the Truth)

📖 Perhaps you've wondered, *What's the big deal about sex outside of marriage? Lots of people do it! Why is this so important to God?*

It's important because He created our bodies, and He designed them to unite with one person—our spouse, in a pure, sexual relationship. He knows that by design, our bodies are physically incapable of fighting off certain germs, bacteria, and diseases transmitted through sexual activity, diseases that will harm us and our ability to fulfill His commandment to "be fruitful and increase in number," which means have sex and make babies! He forbids certain sexual activities, because He wants to help us maintain sexual health and relational happiness.

The bottom line is that God wants the very best for us, and He lovingly communicates to us through Scripture that sex outside of a marriage relationship is not His plan and can be very dangerous. 📖

7. If God wants us to be happy, why doesn't He allow us to have sex anytime we want with anyone we want?

📖 Every time you choose to passionately kiss or touch a guy in a sexual way, you are sending a message that he can treat you like his little plaything. Every time you hold on to your boundaries, you teach him that you are a young woman of integrity who is worth the wait. If he is too impatient to wait until marriage, then *he's* risky marriage material anyway. If you are too impatient to wait until marriage, you are learning patterns that make you risky marriage material too. You want to be able to trust each other wholeheartedly, and dating is a season in which you earn that trust. He will either prove himself to be a young man of integrity and a good candidate for a lifelong, committed marriage, or he will prove himself to be a selfish man of compromise who probably couldn't control his sexual passions even with a wedding band on his finger. 📖

8. If a guy makes a move on you and tries to get physical, should you be flattered because he thinks you are irresistible, or offended because he thinks you're willing? How will you respond if this actually happens to you?

9. What does it say about a guy's character if he treats you in a sexual way? Would this be the kind of guy you'd like to commit your life to? Why or why not?

❧ GROWING TOGETHER
(Sharing the Truth in Small-Group Discussion)

> 📖 Over the past several decades, many have come to view sex as an extracurricular activity, just another pleasurable pastime. Many young women tell us that it's now popular to "hang out and hook up," have "friends with benefits," or be "booty buddies." In other words, sex without any commitment expressed or expected. They meet, they mate, and they walk away to find their next "hookup." 📖

10. What would you say to a close friend who chose to get involved in a sexual "hookup" with no commitment?

📖 If at any point you sense a radar alarm going off in your spirit that says, *WARNING! This doesn't feel right!* listen to it. Don't ignore your mind or your heart telling you to slow down. Let your conscience be your guide. God put that radar there. You may have ignored it in the past, but you can learn to listen for it again. If things get a little too close to compromise, let that radar guide you and resist doing things that make you uncomfortable or that you feel may be wrong. If you ignore those warnings, you may become desensitized to them when they are alerting you to real danger. But if you submit to your radar and let it be your guide, it will keep you safe.

When that radar begins to get your attention, simply smile and say to your boyfriend, "I'd prefer you not do that, okay?" You don't have to be offensive, just invite him to support your boundaries. If he continues to push your boundaries, trying to get you to do things you don't feel comfortable doing, get offensive if necessary. Let him know that if he can't respect you, he can't spend time with you. Remember, no one else can guard your body and your sexual purity. That's your job. 📖

11. Has your warning radar ever gone off because you were about to do something that didn't feel right? If so, how did you respond?

12. If you have ignored your warning radar in the past and done things you wish you hadn't, how can you develop a renewed sensitivity to it and allow your conscience to be your guide once again?

13. *Every Young Woman's Battle* encourages you to refrain from the following sexual activities:

deep, passionate (French) kissing   breast stimulation

full-body hugs   mutual masturbation

sitting in a guy's lap   oral, anal, or vaginal sex

Why would refraining from these sexual activities provide your romantic relationships with a sense of safety?

14. Could the list be adjusted in any way and still ensure safe boundaries and sexual integrity? Why or why not?

∞

Dear Lord, help us to establish and maintain healthy physical boundaries for the sake of our own health and the health of our future children. Teach us to behave and respond in healthy ways with our brothers in Christ, and give us the courage and compassion to speak the truth in love to our sisters as well. Give us open minds to receive Your wisdom through the mouths of others, and keep our hearts soft to Your loving guidance and direction. In Jesus' name. Amen.

looking for love
in the right places

Read chapters 23–25 of *Every Young Woman's Battle*

🪴 PLANTING GOOD SEEDS
(Personally Seeking God's Truth)

As you seek to understand the true nature of love, plant 1 Corinthians 13:4-8 in your heart:

> Love is patient, love is kind. It does not envy, it does not
> boast, it is not proud. It is not rude, it is not self-seeking, it
> is not easily angered, it keeps no record of wrongs. Love does
> not delight in evil but rejoices with the truth. It always pro-
> tects, always trusts, always hopes, always perseveres. Love
> never fails.

1. When you become involved in a serious relationship—or if you already are—how can this verse help you evaluate how healthy your relationship is or how well you treat each other?

As you seek to make Jesus Christ the first love of your life, plant these good seeds in your heart:

> But seek first his kingdom and his righteousness, and all these things will be given to you as well. (Matthew 6:33)

> Delight yourself in the LORD
>   and he will give you the desires of your heart.
>   (Psalm 37:4)

2. What do you think it means to put God first? How can you delight in Him? Will anything in your life need to change in order for you to do this? Explain your answer.

If you wonder if you can really enjoy a deeper, more intimate love relationship with God, plant this seed in your heart:

Ask and it will be given to you; seek and you will find; knock and the door will be opened to you. For everyone who asks receives; he who seeks finds; and to [her] who knocks, the door will be opened. (Matthew 7:7-8)

3. If you try to have a more fulfilling relationship with God, what does this verse say will happen? How could you test God on this?

⚒ WEEDING OUT DECEPTION
(Recognizing the Truth)

📖 Does God have only one guy for you? Can only one man be your soul mate? Of course not. God does not cruelly hide Mr. Right somewhere on the planet, and then say, "Okay, now you have to find him!" Many young men could qualify as your Mr. Right, but you get to choose which one you want to commit to. However, even if you do not choose wisely and marry Mr. Wrong, when you recite your wedding vows, he automatically becomes your Mr. Right. It's God's will that you be a committed wife to this man, through good times and bad, regardless of the character flaws that may surface down the road. If you're wise you'll enjoy the exploration season for many years so that you can truly discern the best match for you. 📖

4. What would you say to a young woman who believes that only one guy can be her Mr. Right and that marrying anyone else besides this "magical one" would be disastrous?

5. How does knowing you can't get a "refund or exchange" on a husband affect the time you take in looking for Mr. Right and getting to know him as best you can before you say, "I do"?

📖 *Practice delayed gratification by not living together, and resist any type of sexual involvement.* In a *Christianity Today* poll, 70 percent of teens overall and 50 percent of Christian teens said they thought living together prior to marriage (cohabitating) was perfectly acceptable.[1] Many young women attempt to secure their relationship with a guy by becoming sexual with him, thinking that if she gives him her body, he'll never leave. *Don't be fooled.* Remember, what a guy usually wants most is sex, and if he's already getting sex, why should he give up his freedom and get married?. . . Good things come to those who wait, and a sexual relationship is well worth the wait. Delaying sexual gratification now can set your marriage up for a lifetime of sexual gratification later. 📖

---

1. "Weekly Illustration Update," Sunday, August 10, 2003, www.preachingtoday.com.

6. Why isn't it wise to live together or to have sex prior to marriage? List every reason you can think of.

    📖 If you have asked Jesus to live inside your heart, He wants to live there permanently, not just rent a room there during the seasons that you don't have a boyfriend. Don't force God to take a backseat to anyone. Keep guys in their rightful place in your heart, and make sure you keep Jesus as your first love. Of course God wants you to love other people, but not more than you love Him. 📖

7. In what ways do young women often make God take a backseat to their boyfriends?

8. What are some practical ways you can guard against doing this in your own life? How can you keep Jesus as your first love?

🐚 HARVESTING FULFILLMENT
(Applying the Truth)

> 📖 *How do I know if it's really love?* This question reflects the
> wrong belief that love is a feeling. Most married couples will
> tell you that some days they "feel" like they are in love and
> other days they don't feel like it at all. Feelings are fickle, but
> love is not a feeling. Love is a commitment. So if you want
> to know if you really love a particular guy, ask yourself, "Am
> I really committed to this person?" If not or if your commit-
> ment is conditional, then you don't love him. If you are
> committed to loving that person unconditionally, even on
> the days that you find it difficult, then yes, it's love. 📖

9. Why do you think love is not as much a feeling as it is a commitment?

10. How could remembering the previous passage help you stay in love
    and committed to your husband?

📖 God extends to us an eternal commitment of love, a love so deep, so wide, and so great that we cannot possibly fully understand it. This gift should inspire us to reciprocate with as equal a gift of love as is humanly possible. What started out as an engagement relationship between God and His own in the Garden of Eden will come to fullness at the wedding supper of the Lamb when Jesus Christ returns to claim His bride, the church.

So how can you cultivate a bridal love for Jesus and enjoy this intimate relationship that He longs to have with you? By falling in love with Him and attempting to pursue Him as passionately as He has been pursuing us all along. 📖

11. How does it make you feel to know that Jesus Christ has chosen *you* as *His* bride?

12. How can you begin to pursue Jesus as passionately as He has been pursuing you all along? List as many ways as you can think of.

❧ GROWING TOGETHER

(Sharing the Truth in Small-Group Discussion)

13. Which of the four seasons of life are you currently in?

___ The Exploration Season

___ The Consideration Season

___ The Commitment Season

___ The Cementing Season

14. Is this an enjoyable season for you? Share with the group why you feel the way you do.

15. What changes in your life need to take place before you are ready for that next season (grow older, finish high school, give the relationship more time to mature, and so on)?

16. Below is a checklist for how to know if a guy is Mr. Right. Rank each item on a scale of 1 to 10 according to how important each characteristic is to you (1 being extremely important and 10 being not very important):

___ spiritual maturity and Christlike character
___ strong family background
___ financial responsibility
___ vision for the future
___ physical attractiveness

What other qualities should be added to this list?

17. To follow are the ten characteristics that young men generally look for in Mrs. Right. For each, rate yourself on a scale between 1 ("I am that woman!") and 10 ("I need help!"):

___ She loves God and has a personal relationship with Jesus Christ.
___ She takes care of herself and has a positive self-image.
___ She is generally a happy person and has a positive outlook on life.
___ She exercises self-control around other guys.
___ She is careful with money and can budget wisely.
___ She has good relationships with her family and has close friends.
___ She is nurturing and would make a good mother someday.
___ She is supportive of what her husband wants to do with his life.

____ She is well educated and has her own dreams and goals.

____ She is adventurous and can enjoy other people's hobbies.

Circle the characteristics (in the previous list) that you need to strengthen before you are ready to be anyone's Mrs. Right. How do you intend to go about strengthening them?

18. Which of the following metaphors describes the level of intimacy you have with Jesus Christ? Circle one.

Potter / Clay Relationship
Shepherd / Sheep Relationship
Master / Servant Relationship
Friend / Friend Relationship
Father / Daughter Relationship
Groom / Bride Relationship[2]

19. Share some ways you could move to a deeper level of intimacy with God.

---

2. Prepared by Jack Hill to encapsulate the points made in Craig W. Ellison, "From Eden to the Couch," *Christian Counseling Today* 10, no. 1 (2002): 30. Used with permission.

20. If you don't feel inspired to do these things right now, what would it take to encourage you? If you want to ask someone to hold you accountable to pursuing a deeper level of intimacy with Jesus Christ, do so now.

∞

Lord, we trust that only You know when the time is right for Mr. Right. Help us to be patient and enjoy each season of our lives. Teach us even now in our family relationships and friendships how to be good companions in preparation for marriage someday. But most of all, Lord, give us a heart that longs after You and show us how to make You our first love. Thank You for the time that we've enjoyed studying Your words together over the past eight weeks, and help us remain strong in guarding our minds, hearts, and bodies. Thank You for guaranteeing us victory in this battle against sexual compromise. In Your most holy and precious name we pray. Amen.

don't keep it to yourself

Congratulations on finishing this workbook! You are well on your way to winning the battle for sexual and emotional integrity. I pray that you have learned how to guard not just your body but your mind and heart from sexual compromise. Most of all, I hope you have tasted and seen that, in fact, the Lord is good and His plans are perfect.

If you've just completed the *Every Young Woman's Battle Workbook* on your own and benefited from it, let me encourage you to consider inviting a group of other young women together and leading them toward guarding their mind, heart, and body as well. This can help keep you accountable, but it will also enable you to encourage and help others who are in the battle with you. If we can encourage each other to open up about our struggles in this area, we will be able to get the support and help we need.

You'll find more information about starting such a group on pages 2–3 of "Questions You May Have About This Workbook."

about the author

Shannon Ethridge is a wife, mother, writer, speaker, lay counselor, and missionary for sexual integrity. Speaking to youth, college students, and adult women since 1989, her passions include instilling sexual values in children at an early age, challenging young people to embrace a life of sexual purity, ministering to women who have looked for love in all the wrong places, and challenging all women to make Jesus Christ the primary Love of their life.

A regular instructor on the Teen Ministries Mania campus, Shannon has been featured numerous times on radio and television programs. She and her husband, Greg, have been married for fourteen years and live in a log cabin among the piney woods of east Texas with their two children, Erin (twelve) and Matthew (nine).

Shannon Ethridge
Ministries

For speaking engagements or other resources available through Shannon Ethridge Ministries, go to www.shannonethridge.com or e-mail Shannon at SEthridge@shannonethridge.com.

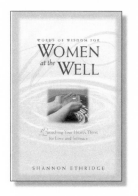
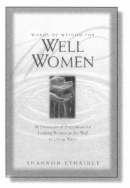

guys aren't the only ones fighting a battle for purity

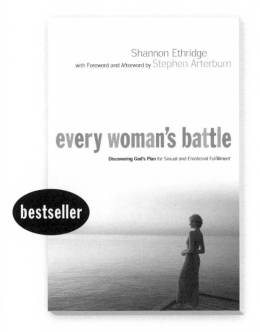

Women, like men, are fighting dangerous sexual battles. The only way you as a woman can survive the intense struggle for sexual integrity is by guarding not only your body, but also your mind and heart. From the coauthor of the Every Man series, Stephen Arterburn, and best-selling author Shannon Ethridge, *Every Woman's Battle* and *Every Young Woman's Battle* are designed to challenge and equip women of all ages to live sexually and emotionally pure lives.

Protect your sexual integrity and live your life to the fullest—without regrets.

Available in bookstores everywhere.

every man's battle workshops

from New Life Ministries

new Life Ministries receives hundreds of calls every month from Christian men who are struggling to stay pure in the midst of daily challenges to their sexual integrity and from pastors who are looking for guidance in how to keep fragile marriages from falling apart all around them.

As part of our commitment to equip individuals to win these battles, New Life Ministries has developed biblically based workshops directly geared to answer these needs. These workshops are held several times per year around the country.

- Our workshops **for men** are structured to equip men with the tools necessary to maintain sexual integrity and enjoy healthy, productive relationships.

- Our workshops **for church leaders** are targeted to help pastors and men's ministry leaders develop programs to help families being attacked by this destructive addiction.

Some comments from previous workshop attendees:

"An awesome, life-changing experience. Awesome teaching, teacher, content and program."   —DAVE

"God has truly worked a great work in me since the EMB workshop. I am fully confident that with God's help, I will be restored in my ministry position. Thank you for your concern. I realize that this is a battle, but I now have the weapons of warfare as mentioned in Ephesians 6:10, and I am using them to gain victory!"   —KEN

"It's great to have a workshop you can confidently recommend to anyone without hesitation, knowing that it is truly life changing. Your labors are not in vain!"   —DR. BRAD STENBERG, Pasadena, CA

If sexual temptation is threatening your marriage or your church, please call **1-800-NEW-LIFE** to speak with one of our specialists.

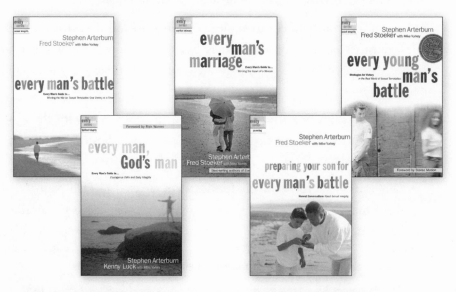